Know God
Published by Orange, a division of The reThink Group, Inc.
5870 Charlotte Lane, Suite 300
Cumming, GA 30040 U.S.A.

The Orange logo is a registered trademark of The reThink Group, Inc.

All Scripture quotations, unless otherwise noted, are taken from the *Holy Bible, New International Version®. NIV®.* Copyright © 1973, 1978, 1984 by International Bible Society. Used by permission of Zondervan.

Other Orange products are available online and direct from the publisher. Visit our website at www.WhatIsOrange.org for more resources like these.

ISBN: 978-0-9890213-0-2

©2013 The reThink Group, Inc.

reThink Conceptual Team:
Ben Crawshaw, Kristen Ivy, Reggie Joiner, Cara Martens, Dan Scott
Lead Writer: Ben Crawshaw
Editing Team: Sarah Anderson, Holly Crawshaw, Jamey Dickens, Laurin Makohon, Lauren Terrell, Jennifer Wilder
Art Direction: Ryan Boon
Design: FiveStone

Printed in the United States of America
Second Edition 2013

2 3 4 5 6 7 8 9 10

03/31/14

KNOW

GOD

DON'T READ THIS BOOK

DON'T READ THIS BOOK.

Wait, wait. That came out wrong. Of course you should read this book. But don't *just* read this book.

Write in it. Draw on it. Mark it up.

If you've never written in a book, today's the perfect day to start.

If you're not a write-in-your-book kind of person, don't sweat it.

Text yourself your thoughts instead.

AND

Find someone else to text and talk to about this book.

Think of one person you know who loves God.
Make sure it's someone you feel comfortable talking to.

Your dad? Small group leader? Student pastor? Orthodontist?

You choose.

Okay. Got someone in mind?

Good. Now, here's the most important thing you will do with this book:

TEAR OUT THIS PAGE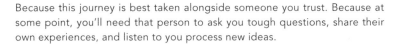
and give it to that person.

Because this journey is best taken alongside someone you trust. Because at some point, you'll need that person to ask you tough questions, share their own experiences, and listen to you process new ideas.

What's up?

I just got a journal called **Know God**. I wanted to tell you about it because you seem like you **Know God**. And even though this is a pretty cool book, it won't be able to tell me everything I need to know about **Know**ing God. So when I handed you this page, it was my way of asking you if we can talk through this together.

So . . . can you help me out?

This journal has devotions for 28 days. That's four weeks. I'm not sure I'll be able to do every single day, but I'm going to give it my best shot. Do you think you can encourage me to stick with it? And if I get off track, can you challenge me to get back on?

Yes? No? Maybe?

One more thing. At the end of each week, can we get together and talk through what I'm learning? I might have some questions. And I believe you'll have some questions for me, too. (That was a hint: there are some questions on the back of this page that might be helpful to ask when we get together.)

I really appreciate your influence in my life. I'm excited about the next four weeks. Thanks for walking through them with me.

Sincerely,

_____

Once again, thanks for hanging out with me for the next four weeks. Any time we get together, feel free to ask me things like:
What's the most interesting thing you read this week?
Was there something that you had a question about?

But, more specifically, here's what I'll be learning. Let's start by talking about this.

WEEK ONE

This week, I discovered that in order to **Know God,** I need to **HEAR** from God.

I LEARNED THAT:

» Creation points to the Creator.
» Jesus' words reveal God's heart.
» The Bible is God's Word.
» The Bible gives our lives direction.
» Reading the Bible is a good habit.
» Memorizing Scripture changes us.
» The Holy Spirit is God's stamp of ownership.

When we get together this week, ask me if I have a plan for reading God's Word. Maybe we could even come up with one together.

WEEK TWO

This week, I discovered that in order to **Know God,** I need to **PRAY** to God.

I LEARNED THAT:

» Prayer helps us get to **Know God.**
» God loves authentic prayers.
» Prayer reminds us who God is.
» God moves when we ask Him to take the lead.
» Prayer reminds us that we need God.
» God forgave us so we should forgive others.
» I have access to God—any time, any place.

When we get together this week, ask me about my prayers. Maybe you could even share one thing you have discovered about prayer in your own life.

WEEK THREE

This week, I discovered that in order to **Know God,** I need to **TALK** about God.

I LEARNED THAT:

» We all need support from good friends.
» I should talk about who Jesus is.
» I can cheer others on in their faith.
» God reveals Himself through our questions.
» I don't have to know everything in order to share what I do know.
» I am created to be a light in the darkness.

When we get together this week, ask me when—and with whom—I am talking about my relationship with God (other than "right now" and "with you").

WEEK FOUR

This week, I discovered that in order to **Know God**, we need to **LIVE** a life that honors God.

I LEARNED THAT:

» God is worth our worship.
» God's love is free.
» God loves it when we give generously.
» The way to find life is to give it away.
» My work is an act of worship.
» When I trust God, I will rest.
» I should start with love.

When we get together this week, ask me how I am worshiping God in the way I live. Maybe we can think of some new ways we could both give, serve, and love others.

KNOWING GOD IS A
LOT LIKE KNOWING
ANYONE ELSE—YOU CAN
LEARN A LOT ABOUT
THEM, BUT THEY STILL
SURPRISE YOU EVERY
NOW AND THEN.

HOW DO I KNOW GOD?

Knowing God doesn't happen in a moment. It's not like you wake up one morning and *BAM*, you **Know God.** You have Him all figured out—everything there is to know. No more questions or doubts.

It doesn't work like that.

Chances are, if you talked to people who believe in God and have known Him for a long time, 100 percent of them would tell you they're still discovering new things about Him. They still have questions. God is still mysterious to them.

Go ahead. Ask them. See what they say.

Knowing God is a lot like knowing anyone else.
You can learn a lot about them, but they still surprise you every now and then.
They aren't puzzles to be solved. Or textbooks to be read.
They're *people* to hang out with.

Knowing God is the same way.
Knowing God is about a RELATIONSHIP.

You can read every word in this book, fill in every blank, follow every suggestion, and still not understand all there is to know about God. And that's okay. Because this book isn't about knowing everything there is to know about God. It's about a journey. A journey where you will—

learn new things.
un-learn what you thought you knew.
connect with a God who already loves you more than you will ever comprehend.

But before you go any further.
Before you even turn to the next page.
There is one thing you absolutely must know about knowing God.

If you want to **Know God,** start with Jesus.

Okay, that's a pretty predictable thing to say. But really, Jesus is the place to start. Why? Well, because Jesus *is* God.
But Jesus was also a man.
He was born.
He had a mother.
She gave Him chores and a curfew. (Maybe.)

He had birthdays. We don't know how He celebrated them, but He had them.

He ate,
slept,
got thirsty,
sneezed.
The list could go on and on.

Jesus was literally God walking around on earth—just like you. So what Jesus said . . . yeah, those are God's words. And what He did . . . well, that should give us a pretty good idea of what God is like.

So, if you really want to Know God, get to know Jesus.

HOW DO I KNOW JESUS?

That's the next logical question, right? Jesus isn't exactly sending you texts, retweeting you, or sharing pics on Instagram. (Although, if He did, that would make for an awesome story).

So, how do we get to know Him?

If you want to know Jesus, read His story.

Jesus' story is the Bible. Maybe you have a Bible that your grandma gave you seven years ago. Or maybe you have a fancy app that lets you search funny verses about donkeys. But let's be honest, other than settling an argument or answering a question at church, how much have you interacted with the Bible?

You may not know this, but the Bible is not a book. It looks like a book. You can flip through it like a book. You can download it like a book.

But it's really not one book.
It's 66 books,
written by 40 authors
over 1,600 years.
And it all comes together to tell ONE STORY.

It's not just any story. It's a story about—
A really big God who loved sinful people
SO MUCH
that He became a human.

Jesus.

And Jesus
lived,
died,
and rose again,
so WE could be forgiven
and live with Him forever.

This is the story that helps us know Jesus.
This is the story that gives us context for everything we know about God.

⊙ HERE ARE A
FEW THINGS WE
KNOW ABOUT GOD
BECAUSE OF HIS
STORY:

» We **Know God** is good because He created a perfect world.
» We know bad things will happen because when people rebelled against God, the world became broken.
» We **Know God** won't abandon us because we see how He pursued sinful and disobedient people for thousands of years.
» We know we can trust God to keep His promises because He already kept His greatest promise by sending His Son.
» We know we can be forgiven because Jesus died for us and already took on all the punishment for our sin.
» We know that one day we can live with God in heaven because Jesus defeated death once and for all.
» We know that until we live with God face-to-face, we are called to live a life that is characterized by love, because that's what Jesus taught.

THE
BIG IDEA.

You getting it so far? Let's review.
You want to **Know God?** Great!
Start by getting to know Jesus.
The best way to know Jesus is to read His story—the Bible.
Specifically, the part where He shows up on the scene.

In other words, start by reading the Gospels (Matthew, Mark, Luke, John).
Four different accounts written by four different men.
All about what Jesus said and did.

But even before you read the Gospels, you might be interested to know there is one thing Jesus did that is more important than anything else.

You can probably guess what it is. He died for the sins of the world, and after three days, He rose from the dead—not like some-zombie-in-a-video-game alive again, but like, walking-around-eating-breakfast-with-His-friends alive again.

Jesus died. He rose to life again. He's alive. And that's the most important thing He did.

But there was also something significant that Jesus *said*.
Okay, *everything* He said was significant. *Really* significant.
But there was one thing He said that was more important than anything else.
Not according to us. According to Him.
Of all the things Jesus said, this one thing is key to **Know**ing **God**.

Jesus said this one thing on a day when a group of religious leaders—men who had spent their entire lives studying God—approached Him and one of them asked Him this question:

"Teacher, what is the most important commandment in the law?"

Check out what Jesus said:

"'Love the Lord your God with all your heart and with all your soul and with all your mind.' This is the first and greatest commandment. And the second is like it: 'Love your neighbor as yourself.' All the Law and the Prophets hang on these two commandments," (Matthew 22: 37-40).

That's it.
The most important commandment.
The biggest idea.
Everything else that the Bible teaches comes back to this.
If you start to understand these 48 words now,
you can worry about the other hundreds of thousands of words in the Bible later.

Because really, it's pretty simple.
The most important thing you could ever do is **Love God.**

And if you aren't sure how to love God, a good way to start is by loving the people He loves:
God loves *you.*
And God loves *others.*

You can know for sure that God loves *you* because He created you. And He cared enough about you to show up on this planet to die for you so you can be forgiven and be with Him forever.

And you can know for certain that God loves *others* because, guess what, He created them and died for them, too. All of them. The people you'd give your last stick of gum to and the people who make you want to move to the South Pole.

It's like Jesus summed up everything you need to know by saying: *It's about three relationships. God. Self. Others.*

OR IF YOU WANT TO SIMPLIFY IT EVEN MORE, IT'S ABOUT ONE IDEA:

LOVE.

Love God.
Love yourself the way He loves you (which is a lot, by the way).
Love others the way He loves them.

That's where Jesus started. So as you begin this journey, it makes sense for you to start there, too.

TO SUM IT ALL UP

1

When you get to know
GOD'S STORY,
it helps you
understand your own
story. (You know more
about yourself because
you understand more
about the One who
made you).

2

Then as you understand
YOUR STORY,
it helps you see how
you're connected to
the stories of others.

3

So, the way to
begin living out
OUR STORY
is to love others the
way that God loves.

SEE HOW THAT WORKS?

FOUR WAYS TO KNOW GOD EVERY DAY . . .

EVEN THOUGH THERE'S NO FORMULA FOR KNOWING EVERYTHING ABOUT GOD, THERE ARE A FEW THINGS YOU CAN DO EVERY DAY THAT WILL HELP YOU KNOW HIM BETTER.

HEAR

PRAY

If you want to know someone, what's one of the first things you do? You listen. Guys, good luck getting a girl to agree to a second date if you don't listen to what she says. Girls, if you're dating a guy who never listens to you, stop! Why is listening so important? Because *that other person* is the only one who can tell you what he or she is thinking and feeling, what makes him or her laugh or get angry. The same is true for God. If you want to **Know God,** you have to learn how to listen. And when you get in the habit of hearing from Him, it helps you *trust* Him more.

Have you ever been in a relationship where the other person did ALL the talking? That's weird, right? God thinks so, too. He doesn't want a relationship with you where He's the only one talking. Sure, He has moments where He just wants you to be quiet and listen. But for the most part, He wants you to talk back. He wants to hear from you—your frustrations, worries, fears, dreams, requests, and interests. So if you want to **Know God,** get in the habit of talking with Him. Because when you pray, it *connects* you with God.

THAT'S WHAT THIS JOURNAL IS ALL ABOUT—FOUR THINGS THAT YOU CAN DO TODAY (AND EVERY DAY) THAT WILL HELP YOU **KNOW GOD.**

TALK

LIVE

Who is your closest friend? Do you talk about that person when he's not around? Sure you do. Not in a bad, trash-talking kind of way. In a good way. You talk about the parkour flip he did off a brick wall. You talk about the hilarious joke she told. You talk about where you hung out this weekend. In fact, you probably hang out with people who also like hanging out with your friend. The same is true with God. As you get to know Him, you'll find that you want to talk about Him more. You want to be around other people who talk about Him. And when you talk about Him—and listen to others talk about Him—it helps you *see* Him in new ways.

Have you ever had someone give you a gift or do something for you that was ridiculously nice? Like, so unbelievably amazing that you just *had* to find a way to thank them? The same is true with God. As you get to **Know God** more, you will discover more and more about how awesome He is. Don't be surprised if you find yourself wanting to say *thank you* in your own unique way. Maybe you'll respond by singing, jumping up and down, silently thinking about Him, painting a picture, serving the homeless, or volunteering to help kids at your church. Regardless of how you do it, the more time you spend with God, the more you will want to respond to His awesomeness by *honoring* God with your life.

HEAR

HEAR

If you want to **Know God,** the first thing you want to do is hear from Him. But how do you hear from Someone who isn't likely to—
walk onto your school campus?
sit next to you at lunch?
send you a text?
ride in your car?
or hang out with you on a Friday night?

How do you hear from Someone that you can't even see?

Actually, the Bible gives us a pretty good clue. It says this:

> *"No one has ever seen God, but God the One and Only, who is at the Father's side, has made him known," (John 1:18).*

The One and Only who is at the Father's side. That's Jesus. There it is again—this idea that **if you want to Know God, get to know Jesus.** Jesus is the best way to **Know God** because Jesus walked around on this planet and *showed us what God is like*. He's not physically here now, but He was here. And while He was here, He spent a lot of time with 12 guys who are sometimes called *disciples* and sometimes called *apostles*. Call them whatever you want. The point is they got to know Jesus pretty well.

They were there when Jesus taught.
They were there when Jesus did some incredible miracles.
They were there when Jesus died.
And all of them (except Judas) were there to see Him alive once again after He rose from the dead.

They were also around for another important event that happened after Jesus rose from the dead—He *ascended*. Meaning, one minute He's chillin' on a hill outside Jerusalem, and the next minute He's floating up into the sky until He disappears. (Now, *that* would be cool to see!)

So, why does it matter that these guys witnessed so much of Jesus' life and ministry? And what does that have to do with hearing from God?

A lot.

Right before Jesus ascended, He gave His friends their most important mission: Go. Tell people what you've seen and heard.

> *"You will be my witnesses in Jerusalem, and in all Judea and Samaria, and to the ends of the earth," (Acts 1:8).*

And guess what? They did.

They went. They told. Some of them wrote it down.

Two of Jesus' disciples documented everything they knew about Him. Think about it—these guys *knew* Jesus. He was their friend, wingman, bro, amigo, bff, bffl, blt. Okay, that last one is a sandwich, but you get the point. When the disciples wrote about Jesus, they were writing about Someone they had traveled with, eaten with, camped with, and hung out with. They had seen Him in action.

They wrote about His birth. They wrote about how His ministry got started. They put down on paper everything they could remember about what He did and said. You might recognize their names: Matthew and John.

There were two other guys you might be interested to know. Their names were John Mark and Luke. (John Mark is one guy—just two first names. Let's just call him Mark for short.) Mark and Luke weren't in the group of 12 guys who hung out with Jesus, but they knew some of those guys. Mark was friends with one of Jesus' disciples named Peter, and Luke interviewed just about everybody who encountered Jesus. These two guys also wrote about Jesus based on eye-witness accounts.

Today, you can still read the words of Matthew, Mark, Luke, and John. They're the first four books of the New Testament. We call them the Gospels, and each one gives us a unique perspective on the life of Jesus.

If you want to **Know God,** read His story. Think about who He is and what He says. Hearing from God in this way will help you trust Him more.

So, here's one thing to think about as you start this week: **If you want to Know God, remember His words.**

DAY 1

Did you know that 45,000 thunderstorms occur every day? Sounds almost impossible, right? It probably also makes you want to take a nap. Because what's better than a nap during a thunderstorm? No, seriously. What's better?

Wait! Wake up! No napping. (Even if there is a thunderstorm where you are.) Listen to this: According to NASA, you'd have to detonate *100 billion tons* of dynamite *every second* to match the energy produced by the sun. That's insane to think about!

Whether it's clouds, rain, lightning, stars, the sun, the moon, or the expanse of the sky, if you go outside and look *up*, there's a lot going on. But very few of us spend much time looking that direction. (Probably because we're looking down at our phones too much.)

King David, one of the most famous kings of Israel, wrote about *looking up* as a way to Know God. There's a book in the Old Testament called *Psalms*, which means *praise songs*. David wrote several songs. And although you won't hear one of David's psalms on Pandora, you can still appreciate it as good music. Check out this lyric:

> *"The heavens declare the glory of God; the skies proclaim the work of His hands," (Psalm 19:1).*

◑ WHAT DO YOU THINK THIS VERSE MEANS?

....

....

....

Nature *declares* and *proclaims*. **Creation points to the Creator.** It says something. It makes an announcement. The question is, do we hear what nature is saying?

David believed nature made statements about God. Statements like:

God is an astounding Creator.
God's creativity is unending.
The beauty around us reflects God's glory. (Glory = Honor + Awe)

Jesus made a similar observation:

> *"Look at the birds of the air; they do not sow or reap or store away in barns, and yet your heavenly Father feeds them. Are you not much more valuable than they?" (Matthew 6:26).*

Jesus urges us to open our eyes to what's around us. Because by paying attention to *creation*, we can better understand our *Creator*. Even more, we can catch a glimpse of the great love our Creator has for us.

With that in mind, here's a two-part challenge for today:

1. **Look around.** Go outside. Take a walk. Pay attention to creation. Ask yourself, what does this say about its Creator?
2. **Say thanks.** Tell God you appreciate His work. Maybe something like this: *God, thank You for the creativity You put into nature. I know that all creation points back to You. So in seeing this, I appreciate You more.*

Nature makes an announcement about God. The question is, *are we listening?* It's time for us to hear God and **Know God.**

◑ AFTER SPENDING SOME TIME OUTSIDE, WHAT DID YOU LEARN ABOUT GOD?

....

....

....

DAY 2

Before Jesus became famous for being, well, Jesus, He had a job. No, not being the Savior of the world—though He was certainly that. But for a period of time, Jesus had an actual trade job.

Now, there's a good bit of debate about exactly which job He had. But basically, the argument comes down to four professional titles that Jesus possibly held:

1. Carpenter
2. Mason
3. Engineer
4. Handyman

So, which is the correct answer? We have no clue. But one thing we can be sure of is that Jesus was in the construction business—which makes sense in light of a story He told about building a house.

But before we get to that story, take a minute to think about this: What do you think about when you consider what it means to follow God? Does your mind immediately go to *rules*? You know, all the stuff you should and shouldn't do? All the people you should avoid hanging out with? Or maybe the ones you should be nice to, forgive, encourage, help, and love?

🔾 TAKE A MINUTE TO NAME SOME THINGS YOU THINK GOD WANTS YOU TO DO OR NOT DO:

....

....

....

Here's another question: Why *should* you do (or not do) these things? With Jesus' experience in construction in mind, listen to the following excerpt. It will help us answer that question.

"Therefore everyone who hears these words of mine and puts them into practice is like a wise man who built his house on the rock. . . . But everyone who hears these words of mine and does not put them into practice is like a foolish man who built his house on sand," (Matthew 7:24, 26).

Jesus goes on to say that a storm came. The house on the rock took it like a champ. The house on the sand? Crumbled. Destroyed. Woodpile for a bonfire.

Jesus' story tells us:

1. **What** we should do. He makes it as obvious as possible—build your life on Jesus' words. Put them into practice.
2. **Why** we should do it. Not just because our parents or the church says so, but because it's smart. This isn't about a list of rules—this is about creating a foundation that will hold.

Jesus' words reveal God's heart. When you study the words of Jesus, it will help you **Know God** more. But Jesus' words won't really do much until you apply them. When the storms come, you'll be happy you built your homes (lives) on the rock (Jesus' words). It won't keep the storms from happening, but it will make us better equipped to handle them.

◑ WHAT DO YOU WANT TO BUILD YOUR LIFE ON? HOW DO YOU PLAN ON DOING THAT?

....

....

....

DAY 3

Do you yawn a lot? (Are you yawning right now?) Although there are lots of theories about *why* we yawn, none of them have been indisputably proven. The Ancient Greeks believed that yawning was a person's soul trying to escape his or her body. If that's the case, your soul can probably make it to the other side of the world and back by the end of second period.

Another theory is that *boredom* is the cause. If you're having a conversation with someone and he starts yawning, you assume he'd rather be reading the iTunes' terms of service agreement, right?

If boredom is, in fact, the cause of yawning, does the idea of reading the Bible automatically make you yawn? It seems like there's a lot of people who think they *should* read the Bible, but they don't because it's boring. Or old. Or hard to understand.

Let's be honest. There are some parts of the Bible that are less than riveting—like instructions on burnt offerings or dimensions of the temple. Just *thinking* about reading those things probably made you yawn. Twice.

○ TALK ABOUT YOUR HISTORY WITH THE BIBLE. HAVE YOU READ IT A LOT? A LITTLE? NEVER? WHAT DO YOU THINK ABOUT THE BIBLE?

....

....

....

Here's another question: Do you think the Bible is relevant to your life *right now*? Do you believe it has something to say about your family, friends, dating life, grades, etc.?

In the New Testament, there is a letter written by Paul to one of his best friends, Timothy. And in that letter, Paul talks about the idea of Scripture being *alive*:

> *"All scripture is God-breathed and is useful for teaching, rebuking, correcting and training in righteousness, so that the man of God may be thoroughly equipped for every good work" (2 Timothy 3:16-17).*

Paul makes two definitive statements in this verse:

1. **All Scripture is *God-breathed.*** It is inspired by God. It's not just words *about* God—the Bible *is* God's words.

2. **All Scripture is *useful.*** The Bible helps us *know* what is right. But it also helps us *do* what is right. That's the payoff—that we may be *equipped* to follow God's words.

Now, that doesn't mean that you'll never be bored reading the Bible. And it certainly doesn't mean you'll understand it all. But you can trust that **the Bible is God's Word.** For you. And those words are *alive.* If you want to **Know God,** listen to His words in the Bible.

DAY 4

Can you imagine driving a car at night without turning the headlights on? Maybe that sounds cool to you because you're into life-threatening experiences that are likely to get your car totaled. But to anyone with a shred of common sense (or a really nice car) that sounds like a nightmare.

It's true: things are just easier when they're done in the light.

Do ever feel like you're navigating *life* in the dark? You're not sure which way you're supposed to go? You have situations where you wish the answers were clearer?

◑ WHAT ARE SOME AREAS IN YOUR LIFE WHERE MAYBE YOU FEEL LIKE YOU'RE DRIVING IN THE DARK AND YOU WISH YOU COULD GET A LITTLE LIGHT?

....

....

....

The Bible tells us what "light" we need to illuminate the dark areas of life:

> *"Your word is a lamp to my feet a light for my path" (Psalm 119:105).*

If you were hiking on a trail at night and wanted to avoid falling off a cliff, you would hold up a light. Why? So you knew where you were supposed to go. That's what the Bible does—it gives us information so we can see clearly. In other words, **the Bible gives our lives direction.**

Psalm 119 is the longest chapter in the Bible and it's all about God's Word. In fact, the author of the psalm refers to God's Word in almost all 176 verses. And the entire chapter is about how God's words help us avoid *sin*—the things that get us off the track God wants for us. The goal of the chapter? That we would **Know God** better as we allow His words to guide our lives:

🕙 IF YOU WANT TO START READING YOUR BIBLE, BUT YOU AREN'T SURE HOW TO BEGIN, HERE ARE TWO SUGGESTIONS:

1. **Find a good starting place in your Bible.** Don't play Bible Roulette, where you close your eyes and randomly open your Bible to read it. You wouldn't read a normal book like that (or you shouldn't, anyway). Start at the beginning of a book. Here are some good ones to try:

   John
   Mark
   Proverbs
   Psalms
   Philippians

2. **Have a reading goal.** You don't have to understand *everything*. Just read until you understand *something*. Read until you bump into something you can personalize. Here are some questions that might help:

   What does this passage say?
   What does this passage tell me about God?
   How does this passage apply to me right now?

When the Bible begins to illuminate your path, it's exciting! Not only do you begin to **Know God** better, but you begin to trust Him more because you see how His words give your life direction.

DAY 5

Do you have any habits? Do you crack your knuckles? Twirl your hair? Smack your gum? Check your phone every 1.3 seconds? You may need to ask someone who knows you well what your habits are. They may be so habitual that you don't even realize you have them!

The thing about habits is that *bad* ones are a lot easier to establish than good ones.

❂ NAME TWO HABITS THAT YOU'VE FORMED WITHOUT REALLY THINKING ABOUT THEM. (IN OTHER WORDS, NO ONE TOLD YOU TO DO IT; YOU DIDN'T WAKE UP AND DECIDE ONE DAY YOU WERE GOING TO DO IT.)

....

❂ NAME ONE HABIT YOU HAVE THAT'S INTENTIONAL.

....

Reading the Bible is a good habit. Why? Check out this old saying: "First you make your habits, then your habits make you." In other words, reading the Bible will influence who you become.

There are a number of reasons why people don't make reading their Bible a habit:

- They don't have time.
- They're not good at it (meaning they don't know where to start, or they don't understand what they read).
- They don't feel like it.

Those really aren't *reasons* as much as they are excuses.

What if you quit making excuses?

Just like studying, exercising, saving, or practicing, when you read your Bible regularly, you get something in return.

The author of Psalm 1 says it this way:

> *"Blessed is the man who does not walk in the counsel of the wicked. . . .*
> *But his delight is in the law of the LORD, and on his law he meditates*
> *day and night. He is like a tree planted by streams of water which*
> *yields its fruit in season," (Psalm 1:1-3).*

❯ WHAT IS THE MAIN POINT OF THIS PASSAGE?

....

....

....

❯ HOW DOES THIS PASSAGE APPLY TO YOU RIGHT NOW?

....

....

....

Another way of translating the word *blessed* is "happy." "Like a tree planted by streams of water," when you're constantly drinking in God's Word, your character is always being changed for the better—you're always bearing fruit at the right time.

This passage isn't referring to people who only read the Bible when they're in trouble or faced with a desperate decision, it's talking about people who make it a lifestyle—who have a long-term goal of knowing God.

Why don't you try it?

1. **Pick a consistent time.**
2. **Pick a consistent place.**
3. **Make it a habit by committing to 90 days.**

DAY 6

The human brain is an incredible organ. In fact, the brain's memory storage capacity measures around 2.5 petabytes (or a million gigabytes)! That means your brain can hold more data than 15,500 iPhones. Think of it this way: If your brain worked like a digital video recorder in a television, 2.5 petabytes would be enough to hold three million hours worth of television shows. You'd have to leave the television running continuously for more than 300 years to use up all that storage. Try to find a DVR that does that! *Mind*-blowing, right?

❯ KNOWING THIS, WHY DO YOU THINK IT'S SO CHALLENGING TO MEMORIZE SCRIPTURE?

....

....

....

You may ask, "But why is it important to memorize Scripture? It's right there in the Bible to read, so why waste precious brain capacity committing it to memory?" Listen to this:

"I seek you with all my heart; do not let me stray from your commands. I have hidden your word in my heart that I might not sin against you," (Psalm 119:10-11).

Memorizing Scripture changes us. It transforms our minds. When you have God's words in your brain, you quite literally hear from God more often. Your thoughts are more consistently directed *toward* God. And as a result, you'll begin to know Him better.

Do you know the Pledge of Allegiance? Do you know your phone number and address? Do you know the lyrics to at least one Taylor Swift song? (Guys, be honest!) You know these things through *repetition*.

Listen to this: A thought is a physical pathway in the brain. The more you have that thought, the more you groove that path into your mind, and the easier it is to have that thought again. Memorizing Scripture takes work. It takes repetition. But it's possible for every single person who has a brain. (That means you!)

At the end of this section, there's a whole list of great verses for you to memorize. But for today, just start by memorizing *half* of the verse above:

"I have hidden your word in my heart that I might not sin against you."

There. You've seen it. Don't let your smart phone be smarter than you. Memorize some Scripture and see what happens.

DAY 7

According to *ehow.com*, there are six ways to know if you've seen a ghost. Two of those methods include testing electronic appliances and observing the behavior of wild animals in the area. You could probably figure out how to test your appliances. But recording the behavior of wild animals? That sounds scarier than seeing a ghost.

If you're the kind of person who finds ghosts interesting, you should read the Bible. Check this out: When Jesus soared into the sky after His resurrection from the dead, He sent His Ghost to us. Question—*do you still think the Bible is boring?* Because that's straight-up fascinating (and a little freaky) to think about.

Ever heard the term "Trinity"? It refers to the three distinct Persons of God:

1. **God the Father.** He's the Creator of the whole universe. He created the earth and everything in it. When sin entered the world through Adam and Eve's disobedience to Him, God sent a solution to save His creation. He sent:
2. **God the Son.** Jesus. Jesus lived a perfect life, died, and was later resurrected. But when Jesus ascended into heaven, He sent a Helper to those who believed in Him. He sent:
3. **God the Holy Spirit.** This is who we're talking about today. Some people refer to Him as the "Holy Ghost." The Holy Spirit is God's presence that lives in followers of Jesus.

● LOTS OF CHRISTIANS THROUGHOUT HISTORY HAVE DEBATED ABOUT HOW TO DISCUSS OR MAKE SENSE OF THE TRINITY. ONE GOD, BUT THREE PERSONS. WHY DON'T YOU TAKE A SHOT AT IT? HOW WOULD YOU DESCRIBE THE TRINITY?

....

....

....

In 2 Corinthians, the Apostle Paul says this of the Holy Spirit:

"[He] put his Spirit in our hearts as a deposit, guaranteeing what is to come," (2 Corinthians 1:22).

"He" is God.

"Our" includes anyone who believes in Him.

Paul is saying that anyone who believes in God has God's Holy Spirit in their hearts. God's Holy Spirit in us is His way of promising: "You will be Mine forever. Your life will go up and down. You will have good days and bad, but My Spirit in you is the promise I am always here to help you."

Weirded out, yet? Totally confused? That's okay. You don't have to understand the Trinity or even the Holy Spirit to experience God's presence. Just start here: **The Holy Spirit is God's stamp of ownership.**

And when you are reading God's Word and tuned in to His Spirit in your life, you will begin to hear from God in new and exciting ways.

Spend a few minutes praying. Ask God to speak to you through His Spirit inside of you. Ask for His Holy Spirit to give you strength in any struggle you are currently facing.

IF YOU WANT TO **KNOW GOD**. . .
REMEMBER HIS WORDS

||||||||||||||||||||||||||||||||||||||||||||||||||||||||||||||||||||||||||||||||||||||||||||||||||||||||||||||||||||||||||||||||||||||||||||||||||

⊘ THERE ARE LOTS OF VERSES IN THE BIBLE THAT ARE WORTH REMEMBERING. HERE ARE A FEW TO GET YOU STARTED:

(These could be designed to be cut out etc . . . OR designed so a student could take a picture of it to keep on their phone)

"We are God's workmanship, created in Christ Jesus to do good works, which God prepared in advance for us to do,"
   (EPHESIANS 2:10)

"Trust in the LORD with all your heart and lean not on your own understanding; in all your ways acknowledge him, and he will make your paths straight,"
   (PROVERBS 3:5-6)

"Neither height nor depth, nor anything else in all creation, will be able to separate us from the love of God that is in Christ Jesus our Lord,"
   (ROMANS 8:39)

"God so loved the world that he gave his one and only Son, that whoever believes in him shall not perish but have eternal life,"
(JOHN 3:16)

"Therefore, if anyone is in Christ, he is a new creation; the old has gone, the new has come!"
(2 CORINTHIANS 5:17)

"Do not conform any longer to the pattern of this world, but be transformed by the renewing of your mind. Then you will be able to test and approve what God's will is —his good, pleasing and perfect will,"
(ROMANS 12:2)

"If we confess our sins, he is faithful and just and will forgive us our sins and purify us from all unrighteousness,"
(1 JOHN 1:9)

PRAY

PRAY

||||||||||||||||||||||||||||||||||||||||||||||||||||||||||||||||||||||||||||||||||||||||||||||||

Have you ever been friends with someone you never communicated with?

Didn't think so.

If you want to know someone, you talk with them. You say things and they listen. They say things and you listen. It's just how we're wired to connect with each other.

The same is true when it comes to God. If you want to **Know God,** you pray to Him. And here's the really great news. Because of Jesus, you aren't praying to some far-off, mysterious, unknown God. You are praying to Someone who really understands.

Here's something you might not know:

Before Jesus came to earth, the Israelites connected with God through priests. The priests would regularly present offerings to God as a sacrifice to cover over the sins of the people. Once a year on the Day of Atonement, the high priest would walk through a curtain into a very holy place in the temple where God's presence dwelled. In that place he would make a sacrifice to cover over *all* the sins of the people.

Kind of complicated, but very symbolic. And very powerful.

On the day that Jesus died (actually in the *moment* Jesus died), the curtain that separated the most holy place in the temple from the rest of the world tore open. The separation between God and man was over! Done. Ended. Finished. Removed. Jesus was the once-and-for-all sacrifice for sin. And because He paid for our sin, He changed the way we connect with God from that moment forward.

Now, that's a reason to jump up and down screaming like a twelve-year-old at a Justin Bieber concert! (Just try not to rip down any curtains in your own house!)

Because the separation between God and us is removed, Jesus now functions as our high priest. The writer of Hebrews says it this way:

> *"We do not have a high priest who is unable to sympathize with our weaknesses, but we have one who has been tempted in every way, just as we are—yet was without sin. Let us then approach the throne of grace with confidence, so that we may receive mercy and find grace to help us in our time of need," (Hebrews 4:15-16).*

Isn't that incredible? **You can connect to God by praying** in Jesus' name.
Through Jesus. Because of Jesus.
Jesus makes it possible for us to be close with God.

And Jesus understands what it's like to—
live on this planet.
feel hurt.
be tempted.

In other words, He understands all your drama, frustration and temptation. He gets it. Not only because He's God and He knows everything. He understands because He walked on this planet and experienced life in a human body. But He did not sin. Instead, He defeated it.

That means you can come to Him. Anytime. Anywhere. Boldly.

And because you've learned some things about Jesus, you already know Who you're talking to. So remember this: **If you want to Know God, pray to Him.** Make it a habit.

Not sure how to start? That's okay. We're about to spend a whole week talking about how you can pray.

DAY 8

Have you ever heard little kids pray? They come up with some pretty bizarre—and hilarious—stuff.

Check out these prayers by some kids in elementary school:

>   *Dear God, are You really invisible or is that just a trick?*
>   *Dear God, did You mean for giraffes to look like that or was it an accident?*
>   *Dear God, I think the stapler was one of Your greatest inventions.*
>   *Dear God, thank You for the baby brother but what I prayed for was a puppy.*

You have to love their honesty. Also, who knew little kids use (and apparently love) staplers?

For the rest of the grown-up world, prayer probably looks a little different. In fact, it's probably safe to say most people's prayers typically center around *desperate requests* or *formal acknowledgements*. In other words, most people pray because they have to or because they think they're supposed to.

Here are the most common places and situations where people pray:

1.   Church
2.   Before meals
3.   Funerals
4.   Hospitals
5.   Before tests or exams
6.   Before sporting events
7.   When sporting events come down to the wire
8.   Religious holidays

❍ WHEN DO YOU PRAY? WHAT DO YOU PRAY ABOUT?

....

....

....

If you pray at *all*, great job! That's a big deal! But our prayers should be about more than just tradition or desperation. Prayers should be personal and relational. **Prayer helps us get to Know God.**

Jesus taught one of His most important messages from a mountainside. A large crowd gathered and Jesus began to teach on just about every aspect of life. One of those aspects was prayer:

> *"When you pray, go into your room, close the door and pray to your Father, who is unseen. Then your Father, who sees what is done in secret, will reward you," (Matthew 6:6).*

Jesus is not literally saying that we should only pray in our bedrooms. He's saying that we need to have intentional time where we pray **by ourselves.** God loves it when we get one-on-One with Him because we're more likely to be genuine.

Again, there's nothing wrong with asking God to bless our food or our basketball game. But at its core, prayer is more than that. Prayer is a huge part of our relationship with God. Just think, what would happen if the only thing you said to your friends and family was a quick:

"Thanks for dinner." Or, "Can I borrow a pencil?"

Your relationships would go nowhere fast. **Prayer helps us get to Know God.** And to know *anybody*, you have to spend quality one-on-one time with them— enough time to get past the formalities and requests to the brutal honesty. That's what God is inviting us to do, and that's the secret to a growing prayer life.

Spend five minutes praying. Get by yourself in a private place. Talk to God. Tell Him you want to know Him better.

DAY 9

Did you know that on average we say 10,123 words per day? Guys average a little over 7,000, and girls average well over 13,000. Either *girls* are smarter and their brains are processing more information, or *guys* are smarter and they've learned to keep some thoughts to themselves.

Either way, people have a lot to say.

Maybe that's what you've always thought defined a successful prayer—saying a lot of words. Maybe you thought that the longer the prayer was, the holier it was, and the more likely God would be to respond to it. You've viewed it kind of like a prayer buffet. If you offer enough things, surely God will pick *something* and approve of it.

Or maybe you thought a successful prayer was defined by how good and holy you sounded.

Have you ever heard someone pray and thought, "Wow! *That* was impressive. They should become a professional pray-er. They should enter praying competitions!" because their prayers sound so eloquent? And intelligent? And perfect?

Maybe you try to copy that style of praying because you think, *This is how good prayers should sound.*

Here's a question for you: Do you think your prayers should impress God?

Maybe a better way to ask that question is: Do you believe there is some magic combination of words that makes God listen, respond to, and answer prayers?

But what if prayer wasn't about quality or quantity? What if it was about *authenticity*?

Here's a continuation of Jesus' sermon on prayer:

"When you pray, do not keep on babbling like pagans, for they think they will be heard because of their many words. Do not be like them, for your Father knows what you need before you ask him," (Matthew 6:7-8).

God didn't intend for our prayers to be repetitive and formulaic. You and you're closest friend don't simply repeat the same scripted phrases to each other every time you hang out. Rather, you address each other differently each day, because each day presents unique thoughts, feelings, challenges and situations.

God didn't intend for our prayers to be "holy" auditions. The point of prayer isn't to find all the right words that are impressive to God—the point is to have a real relationship with Him. Instead, **God loves authentic prayers.**

Spend 10 minutes talking to God. Be as real and straightforward as you possibly can. Talk to Him about your secret "stuff"—thoughts, actions and temptations.

DAY 10

Did you know that *octothorpe* is the name of the # symbol on a phone? Doesn't quite have the same ring to it as "hashtag."

Ladies, did you have a Barbie growing up? Did you know that her full name is *Barbara Millicent Roberts*? So regal.

Did you know that there's a town in Georgia named Santa Claus? A Monkey's Eyebrow, Kentucky? And a No Name, Colorado?

Names are a big deal. Branding companies make millions of dollars every year helping businesses come up with the right name. Expectant parents spend countless hours debating potential names for their kids. Imagine a world where no one had a name. Boring, right? And confusing.

It's almost as if our names carry the weight of who we are.

When Jesus talked about prayer during His famous Sermon on the Mount, He gave us an example of how our prayers should look. We creatively call this "The Lord's Prayer." In this prayer, Jesus began with God's name:

> *"This, then, is how you should pray: 'Our Father in heaven, hallowed be your name,'" (Matthew 6:9).*

This introduction to The Lord's Prayer tells us two things:

1. **Start by calling God, "Father."** Just as a child can freely approach a good father, we can approach our perfect Father in heaven. The way we *think about* God affects how we *approach* Him. And the way we approach God is so important that Jesus began His prayer by mentioning it—*approach God as your loving Father.*

   It doesn't mean you have to literally call him *Father* every time you pray. It means simply *acknowledging* that God loves you and will respond to you like a **loving** father would respond to his children.

2. **Continue by honoring His name.** Prayer should start with *God*—not with *us*. God's name carries a lot of weight. He deserves to be recognized and admired. Spend some time thinking about who God is before you starting telling Him everything you need.

Prayer shouldn't just be about us and our wish lists. **Prayer reminds us who God is.**

Take a few minutes and turn your attention to God.

◑ READ PSALM 96 OUT LOUD TO HELP YOU FOCUS ON GOD. WRITE DOWN THREE THINGS YOU ADMIRE ABOUT GOD:

1.
....

2.
....

3.
....

Spend some time in prayer. Thank God for how awesome He is and for all the great things He has done. Talk to Him about the things you wrote down. Read Psalm 96 back to Him.

DAY 11

During World War II, the Japanese military sent Lieutenant Hiroo Onoda to Lubang Island in the Philippines and told him to defend the area at all costs. When the war ended in 1945, Onoda refused to believe it was over. Numerous attempts were made to convince Onoda it was safe to return home, but none were successful. *Twenty-nine* years passed before Onoda surrendered.

Surrender can be a tough concept to embrace, can't it?

Did you ever play the game Say Uncle when you were a kid? Essentially, someone is trying to get you to surrender. And when you do, you say "uncle." Maybe your older brother got you in a torturous headlock and twisted your body into a pretzel, but you simply refused to say "uncle" because you didn't want to give him the satisfaction of winning.

Because that's what surrender means—**"I give up. You win."**

Surrender is tough because we don't like to turn over control to *anybody*. But surrender is important. Surrender has the potential to change your mind, your heart, and your entire life more than anything else. In fact, **surrender is one of the reasons we pray.** This is what Jesus encourages us to pray to our Father in heaven:

> *"Your kingdom come, your will be done on earth as it is in heaven"*
> *(Matthew 6:10).*

See, we are mostly concerned with our little kingdoms: *our* school, team, friends, Instagram followers, family, job, money, dating life, etc. But with this prayer, Jesus is telling us that if we really want God to get involved in our lives, we have to first surrender to His kingdom. In other words, **God moves when we ask Him to take the lead.**

❂ **WHAT ARE YOUR FEARS WHEN IT COMES TO SURRENDERING?**

....

....

....

◆ WHAT FEARS DO YOU HAVE ABOUT ASKING GOD TO TAKE THE LEAD?

....

....

....

◆ WHAT IS ONE AREA OF YOUR LIFE YOU DON'T WANT TO SURRENDER TO GOD? WHY NOT?

....

....

....

It's natural to feel hesitant. But it's important to know that the payoff is incredible. Being surrendered to God is the best place you can possibly be in life! Why? Because you're inviting the *Creator of the universe* to move on *your* behalf. As a result, you get *His* wisdom, power, purpose, heart, creativity, and peace intersecting with *your* everyday life. When you let God win, you win!

Here's what surrendering to God and His kingdom looks like:

WHAT GOD WANTS > WHAT I WANT

Pray the following prayer and then spend some time inviting God to take the lead in specific areas of your life.

*"God, before I pray about **my little kingdoms**, I want to surrender to **Your kingdom.** I want to acknowledge that whatever You want for my life is greater than what I want. I am giving up all of me to all of You. You take the lead."*

DAY 12

Did you know that one flush of the toilet uses up to four gallons of water? Now, we're definitely not trying to debate the appropriate circumstances in which one should or should not flush a toilet. That's just a surprising amount of water. We're talking around 40 gallons of a precious natural resource that you quite literally flush down the toilet each day.

Water is important. You've probably heard a variation of this stat before: You can go three weeks without food, but you can only go *three days* without water. Isn't that strange? Chances are, if you had to choose between a Big Mac and a glass of water, you're going with the Big Mac every time.

But, like it or not, we're all *dependent* on water. You might even say that water *demands* our *dependence*. We have to drink water. We have no choice.

God wants us to be as dependent on Him as we are on water. But He doesn't *demand* our dependence. Instead, He *invites* it.

In Jesus' Sermon on the Mount, He continues The Lord's Prayer with a line about our utter dependence on God:

> *"Give us today our daily bread" (Matthew 6:11).*

"Daily bread" is a reference to a time when the Israelites were literally out of food and God dropped it from the sky every day to keep them alive. *That's* dependence! God says, "Remember when I did that? When you counted on Me to stay alive every day? That's what I want from you right now."

It's okay to ask God for things. In fact, He wants us to do that. But it's important to remember that our asking shouldn't center around what God can do for us—it should center on how much we need Him. Bottom line: **Prayer reminds us that we need God.**

Although there are a lot of ways you can practice dependence on God, let's start with two simple exercises:

1. **Ask God to help you in areas where you're already doing great.** Does that sound weird? It shouldn't. The truth is, all of our talents and skills come from God. And being dependent means claiming our need for Him in areas where it may not appear as obvious that we need Him.

2. **Write down some things you're thankful for.** Thanksgiving reminds us that good things come from God, not from happenstance or good fortune. Here are three benefits of being thankful:
    - » Your mood improves.
    - » Your faith in God increases.
    - » Your perspective changes for the better.

Let's practice:

◑ WRITE DOWN FIVE THINGS YOU'RE THANKFUL FOR, AND THEN SPEND SOME TIME TELLING GOD HOW MUCH YOU NEED HIM:

1.
....

2.
....

3.
....

4.
....

5.
....

DAY 13

What creates happiness? Puppies? Laughing babies on YouTube? Getting a date? Getting rich? According to recent research, **forgiveness** does.

In his article "Forgiveness is Good for Your Health," Gregg Easterbrook says that people who forgive have better health, less depression and better social support than those who don't.

In another study, Everett Worthington, Jr., claims that people who don't forgive have stress problems, immune system problems, and cardiovascular problems at a higher rate than the population as a whole.

In other words, forgiveness makes you happy and unforgiveness makes you sick.

Jesus talked about this concept long before psychologists did. Here's what He said:

> *"Forgive us our debts, as we also have forgiven our debtors,"* (Matthew 6:12).

Forgiveness is hard. It's one of those things you almost have to pray about. When people hurt or offend you, your first response probably isn't to shrug it off and forgive. No, to do that you have to take it to God. And when we talk to God about forgiveness it reminds us of two things:

1. **We need forgiveness.** We do things every day that we know we *shouldn't*. And we neglect to do things that we know we *should*. We think things, do things, and say things that go against what God wants. Yet, He continues to offer us grace and forgiveness.

2. **We need to pass on that same forgiveness.** Once we realize how much we need forgiveness, it's easier to distribute it to other people. Maybe they don't *deserve* forgiveness. Guess what? Neither do we, yet God still offers it

It's a simple concept: **God forgave us, so we should forgive others.** But it can be so difficult. And emotional. And powerful. That's why it's important to get in a habit of forgiving when you pray. Because **God forgave us, we are able to forgive others.**

❯ DO YOU HAVE ANY HURT OR ANGER THAT'S CURRENTLY DIRECTED AT SOMEONE? WHAT WAS TAKEN FROM YOU? IN WHAT WAY WERE YOU WRONGED? WHAT WERE YOU OWED?

....

....

....

❯ NOW SPEND SOME TIME PRAYING.

» CONFESS YOUR SINS TO GOD.
» THANK HIM FOR HIS FORGIVENESS.
» FORGIVE THE PEOPLE WHO'VE WRONGED YOU.

DAY 14

Have you ever had a staring contest with someone? You wait to see which person will be the first to blink. Those 15 seconds can be excruciating. Especially if you wear contacts or have dry eyes. In those cases, 15 seconds feel like 15 hours that are followed by rubbing, blinking, squinting, and making very unattractive faces to recover.

The average person blinks every four to six seconds. That number is affected by your environment, how tired you are, and whether or not you are reading a paragraph about blinking (in which case you probably blink every 1.5 seconds). But every person on planet earth blinks and blinks often. You could even say we blink continually.

In the Bible, Paul tells us to do something else continually. It may surprise you:

> *"Pray continually" (1 Thessalonians 5:17).*

Paul didn't really beat around the bush, did he? He was clear about the expectations he had for Jesus-followers. He encourages us to pray and pray often.

Most of us grew up thinking that prayer was reserved for *specific* times and places—before meals and baseball games, during church, before bed at night. But here's the cool thing about prayer as we see in this verse: **We have access to God—any time, any place.**

Before cell phones were invented, calls could only be made from pay phones or home lines—specific times from specific places. But the reason the profit of the cell phone industry tallies in the trillions of dollars every year is because it breaks that barrier and allows us to access people any time from virtually any place.

That's what prayer does—it allows you instant access to God. You don't have to wait until church. You don't have to wait until you clean up your act. You don't have to wait until school, work or practice is over. You can pray to God—**any time, any place.**

But it takes practice. And that's just what you should do! Each day, take the time to:

1. **Pray for people.** When you have conversations with people throughout the day, say a quick prayer for them in your mind: "God, be with Bradley today. Comfort him as he goes through this tough situation with his family."

2. **Acknowledge and invite.** Before you walk into your next stop—school, practice, rehearsal, work, home, etc.—acknowledge God and invite Him into that place: "God, before I walk into my house, I want You to know that I need You. Help me to remember You while I'm at home tonight."

◑ WHERE ARE SOME PLACES YOU CAN PRACTICE PRAYING CONTINUALLY THIS WEEK? YOUR CAR? THE HALLWAY AT YOUR SCHOOL? YOUR BIOLOGY CLASS?

....

....

....

IF YOU WANT TO **KNOW GOD** . . .
PRAY TO HIM

||||||||||||||||||||||||||||||||||||||||||||||||||||||||||||||||||||||||||||||||||||||||||||||||||||||||||||||

Because of Jesus, you can pray directly to God. Anytime. Anywhere. With boldness. And when you pray, it connects you with God.

There's no magic formula for praying. But there are some things you can keep in mind when you're talking to God:

Pray by honoring God.

Pray with humility.

Pray with gratitude.

Pray with honesty.

Pray for forgiveness.

"Do not be anxious about anything, but in everything, by prayer and petition, with thanksgiving, present your requests to God,"
(PHILIPPIANS 4:6)

TALK

||||||||||||||||||||||||||||||||||||||||||||||||||||||||||||||||||||||||||||||||||||||||||||||||||||||||||||||||||||||||||||||||||||||

Here are two facts about you:
You like to talk about things you like.
You like to hang out with people who talk about things you like.

Isn't that true?

Video games. Boys. Movies. UFC. Breakdancing. Lacrosse. Guitar amps. Robots.
We all have stuff we like to talk about.

Name one thing that you like to talk about:
Name one person you like to talk about it with:

When you talk to _____ about _____,
you probably both discover more about it.

Peter and John were two people who liked to talk about Jesus.

Maybe that seems strange to you. But these were two guys who hung out
with Jesus. In fact, they were in Jesus' inner circle. They knew Him well. And
because they knew Jesus—saw what He did and heard what He said—it made
them want to talk about Him like crazy.

Even after Jesus rose from the dead and ascended into heaven, Peter and
John just kept on talking about Him. In fact, the book of Acts records an
interesting story when they got in trouble for running their mouths about
Jesus. They were standing outside the temple saying stuff like this:

> *"Salvation is found in no one else, for there is no other name under
> heaven given to men by which we must be saved," (Acts 4:12).*

That's pretty cool, right? Not if you were a religious leader from back in
the day. They still weren't convinced that Jesus was who He claimed to be.
So, they threw Peter and John in jail for the night. Imagine if your school
administered a "one-night-in-jail" punishment for talking too much. (Have fun
explaining that one to your parents!)

The next day, the religious leaders told Peter and John they were free to go, as long as they promised to stop talking about Jesus.

What do you think they said?

"We cannot help speaking about what we have seen and heard," (Acts 4:20).

In other words, "Nah, we'll pass on your offer. We know you can throw us back in prison. But we won't stop."

And you thought UFC fighters were tough.

That's pretty amazing. Maybe sometimes you feel like you just can't help talking about clothes, lifting weights, your Jeep, etc. Even if you tried to stop, you just couldn't help yourself. That's how Peter and John felt.

They had heard Jesus teach some remarkable things. They had seen Jesus perform some incredible miracles. Most of all, they were there when Jesus was crucified on the cross. And then they *saw* Jesus alive three days later! They witnessed Him—*alive*—with their very own eyes. Who wouldn't talk about that?

Right about now you might be thinking, *"Sure it was easy for these dudes to talk about Jesus. They got to walk around with Him for a couple years."*

But you know something about Jesus, too! You know what He has done in your life. You know the way He has used others to help you learn more about Him and His love. **The way you've experienced Jesus is something that no one else knows—unless you talk about it.**

The same is true for other people. They know what Jesus has done in their lives. So when you talk about Him together, you both get to *see* something new about who He is. It's like God designed us to learn more about Him by talking with other people about what He's done. Crazy, isn't it?

So here's the one thing to remember: **If you want to Know God, talk about Him with your friends.** If you want to know more about how to do that, you're in luck. That's what this week is all about.

DAY 15

Emperor penguins huddle together when it gets too cold. Cute, right? What's odd is that normally penguins are very territorial—they don't always like hanging out with each other. But huddling is what allows them to survive the brutal winter in Antarctica. Scientists have calculated that by huddling, these little guys use about half the energy they would otherwise. As a result, they don't starve to death and their baby chicks live to see the spring.

Even penguins understand that when times get tough, they need each other. Maybe we could learn a thing or two from them.

On your journey to **Know God,** you're going to run into tough times—setbacks, distractions, mistakes, relational drama, and doubt, just to name a few. Maybe you're in the middle of one of those times right now.

Whatever you're facing, you need other people. **We all need support from good friends.** The writer of the book of Hebrews knew the importance of finding support in others during tough times. He knew that in order to keep going, stand strong, and persevere, his readers—the early followers of Jesus—would have to huddle together:

> *"Let us not give up meeting together, as some are in the habit of doing, but let us encourage one another—and all the more as you see the Day approaching," (Hebrews 10:25).*

This verse highlights our need for **community with other Christians.** The author of Hebrews calls it "meeting together." As you get to **Know God** more, you'll encounter confusing aspects of Christianity, church, and the Bible along with the everyday, normal challenges of life. You need people with whom you can process these situations and emotions.

Emperor penguins know it—there is safety in numbers. You need support. You need conversations with and encouragement from other Christians. You need people in your life who want to **Know God,** and who want *you* to **Know God.**

Otherwise, you may find your relationship with God frozen like an emperor penguin standing solo on a glacier in Antarctica in the middle of the winter. Okay, that's a little dramatic.

● HERE ARE A FEW QUESTIONS TO DIRECT YOU TOWARD CREATING YOUR OWN HUDDLE OF BELIEVERS:

Do you have 1-2 Christians you like to hang out with? List them here.

1.
....

2.
....

How do you know the friends you listed care about your relationship with God?
....

....

....

Would you be comfortable talking with them about things you're dealing with in your relationship with God? Why or why not?

....

....

....

We'll talk more about the idea of community in the next couple of days. Take some time and ask God to put the right people in your life to support you.

DAY 16

Jesus' life had a pretty big impact on humanity:

» Jesus introduced the concept of human rights.
» Jesus promoted the idea of women having security and support (instead of being viewed as property and being forced to marry).
» Jesus elevated the value and treatment of children.

We could spend days talking about all the ideas Jesus improved or introduced:

Marriage
Family
Education
Morality
Freedom
Work ethic
Art and literature
Christmas
Grape juice and crackers in church

Okay, we may be getting off track. But you get the point. Jesus was a really cool guy who made some pretty significant contributions to our lives even today.

One day, when Jesus was hanging out with His disciples, He asked them an interesting question:

"'But what about you?' he asked. 'Who do you say I am?'" (Matthew 16:15).

Peter took on the role of spokesman for the crew:

"Simon Peter answered, 'You are the Christ, the Son of the living God.' Jesus replied, 'Blessed are you, Simon son of Jonah, for this was not revealed to you by man, but by my Father in heaven,'" (Matthew 16:16-17).

Peter declared something very important. He was saying that while Jesus said some pretty amazing things—including introducing ideas that people had never thought before—Jesus isn't *just* a good guy. He's not just a great teacher, a powerful prophet, or a wise leader. He's not just a humanitarian, creative storyteller, or religious organizer. He is the Son of the one, *true*, living God. He is the Messiah and Savior.

As Peter *talked* about who Jesus is, all of the disciples took a big step forward in their faith. See, even in just saying that Jesus is *the* Son of God, Peter began to see it, believe it, and experience it more.

The same is true for us. When we open our mouths and talk about who Jesus is, it benefits us and the people around us. It reaffirms in our hearts what we know is true. That's why one of the ways you can **Know God** more, is just to talk about who Jesus is.

So, quite simply, **talk about Jesus.** Maybe it's with:

- » A parent
- » A friend
- » A mentor
- » Your small group leader
- » Your student pastor
- » Your grandma

Be creative. Find ways to talk about His life, His words, His impact on humanity, what makes Him stand out among all other humans past and present, and get to **Know God** better in the process!

DAY 17

In 1979, the Special Olympics held their traditional wheelchair race. A thunderstorm broke out during the competition, but the athletes were encouraged to finish anyway. One participant—who was in last place—wrecked on the track and fell out of his chair.

No one came to his aid. Instead, the crowd began cheering wildly for him to get back in his chair. As the crowd's volume and fervor increased, the racer finally managed to get back into his chair and cross the finish line.

After the race, his coach said this: "I've been coaching and working with that boy for over two years, trying to teach him to climb back onto his chair should he ever fall out. This is the first time he's ever made it."

Encouragement is powerful. That athlete didn't get back in his wheelchair because of adrenaline. He did it because *people cheered for him.*

Words are powerful. And as nice as an inspirational story like this is, here's the harsh reality: Critical words outnumber the encouraging ones in our world. For the most part, we cheer *against* each other. We're sarcastic, discouraging, and sometimes, downright mean. We make fun of each other, cut each other down and point out each other's flaws. And whatever the motivation—humor, insecurity, approval—we're hurting each other.

It would be nice if it were way different when it comes to Christian students. But that's probably not the case. Either way, here's what the author of Hebrews says to us:

> *"Encourage one another daily," (Hebrews 3:13).*

Now, this isn't just about saying polite things. It's not about telling girls that their hair looks pretty or liking your friend's pictures on a social media site. This is about encouraging each other with **truth.** In other words, **cheer others on in their faith.** When people fall down, urge them to get back up. Hold them accountable for what they want to do, and what they *don't* want to do. Talk about what God says.

And the writer says to do it *daily*. In other words, make it a habit. Make it an attitude. Make it a lifestyle.

Everybody needs encouragement. And God may be calling *you* to be the person who meets that need in someone's life.

◑ THINK OF TWO PEOPLE WHO NEED TO BE ENCOURAGED IN THEIR WALK WITH GOD RIGHT NOW. WRITE DOWN THEIR NAMES AND 1-2 WAYS YOU CAN ENCOURAGE THEM:

PERSON: ....

ENCOURAGEMENT: ....

....

....

PERSON: ....

ENCOURAGEMENT: ....

....

....

DAY 18

Santa gets a lot of interesting questions.

» A 7-year-old in New York wrote Santa a letter, asking if—because her parents are divorced—he could make a special two-night visit for her (one stop at each parent's house). Hey, it never hurts to ask!

» A 4-year old in Delaware asked Santa if his mommy made him brush his teeth after he ate milk and cookies at every house. Another valid question.

Questions are a part of life. We ask questions to our parents, teachers, siblings, coaches and friends. We ask questions about Trig, how to drive, music, and sports. But for some reason, we hesitate when it comes to our questions about God.

For many of you, as soon as you even *think* about questioning something concerning religion, a voice goes off in your head that says, *"Shhhhh! Don't ask that in church!"*

Despite that, you still have questions—*big* questions. And those questions bother you. But because you're too shy, too afraid people will think you're stupid or too afraid God will be mad at you, you keep them to yourself.

❍ WHY IS IT SO DIFFICULT TO TALK ABOUT YOUR QUESTIONS ABOUT GOD?

....

....

....

Speaking of questions, here's a good one: **Do you believe your faith and your questions can co-exist?**

Jude—who was the younger half-brother of Jesus—didn't believe in Jesus while He was on earth. (Would you believe your brother if he said he was the Son of God?) But he became a believer after the resurrection. And in this letter, he encourages Christians who are dealing with doubts, questions, and confusion. Here's what Jude says:

"Be merciful to those who doubt," (Jude 1:22).

Jude says not to abandon, judge or belittle people who don't have it all figured out. Instead, he tells us to **be merciful.** That is how you should treat others who ask hard questions and that's how your doubts and hard questions should be received as well—with *mercy.*

See, God doesn't see our questions as obstacles. In fact, oftentimes, **God reveals Himself through our questions.** Our tough questions don't keep us from God—they allow us to experience Him in a new way.

WHAT ARE SOME OF YOUR BIGGEST DOUBTS AND QUESTIONS?

....

....

....

You aren't alone in having questions. Lots of students think about these types of questions, but never do anything about them. So, **talk about these questions with some wise Christians.** Because when you do, you might just be surprised by what you learn about God.

DAY 19

Have you ever stopped to think about how weird Halloween is? Probably not, but why don't you give it a shot right now?

. . .

Right? It's weird. Imagine for a minute that you're a foreign exchange student who has visited America and then returned home to a country where they've never heard of Halloween. "Yeah, so, one night a year they all dress up in costumes. The scarier, the better. There's fake blood, chain saws, and masks. Oh, yeah. And then they all walk around, knocking on doors for candy."

It doesn't make sense. And yet we do it in this country every year without ever thinking about how incredibly strange it is.

Maybe that's true for your home, too. Maybe your family has some traditions or practices that could seem strange to someone if they weren't a member of your family. But for your family, *that's* what brings you together. It's the thing that you look back on with warm, fuzzy feelings. Maybe your tradition is to take a family pic at the end of vacation every summer so you can look at it and remember that trip. That's why a lot of traditions exist—to create moments upon which you look back and remember.

In the Old Testament, King David led the Israelites in a celebration because they were moving the ark of the covenant (the symbol of God's presence) to Jerusalem. This had great significance, but for now just know that it was a big deal and they were excited. So, they sang about it:

"Remember the wonders he has done," (1 Chronicles 16:12).

David understood how passionate people were about God in that moment. But he also knew there would come a day when the excitement would wear off. And he wanted people to *remember* **this moment** when they got to **that moment.**

That's important for us to do as well because there will be days, events, experiences, and moments when we *feel* closer to God than others. And in the moments when God doesn't seem as close, God wants us to hold on to the moments when He did. **Remembering what God has done builds our faith.**

God also wants us to *talk about it* because talking about it helps us remember. Just like our traditions remind us of the best times with our families and friends, talking about what God has done builds our faith in Him.

As for today, here are a few ways to help you remember what God has done:

❂ WRITE DOWN THREE THINGS GOD HAS DONE FOR YOU IN THE PAST. OR WRITE DOWN THREE TIMES YOU FELT REALLY CLOSE TO GOD IN THE PAST.

1.
....
2.
....
3.
....

» **Thank God for those moments.**
» **Come back and read them in the moments you feel most distant from God.**

DAY 20

» Is there a reason why crocodiles swallow stones? Supposedly it helps in digestion.
» Is there a reason why honeybees have hairs on their eyes? It helps them collect pollen.
» Is there a reason goats' eyes have rectangular pupils? It gives them greater depth perception, allowing them to see predators.
» Is there a reason camels have a third eyelid? It helps wash sand out of the other two.

When it comes to your relationship with God, it's important to talk about the reason behind it. Because at some point you'll be asked: *"Why?"* Especially if you are a person who is striving to **Know God** better. At some point, **people will notice.** And someone may ask, "Why do you believe what you believe?"

Peter addresses those times when we have an opportunity to talk to people about our relationship with God:

"In your hearts set apart Christ as Lord. Always be prepared to give an answer to everyone who asks you to give the reason for the hope that you have. But do this with gentleness and respect," (1 Peter 3:15).

Now before you break into a cold sweat, understand when Peter says, "always be prepared to give an answer to everyone," he's not saying:

» You have to become a preacher.
» You have to understand every word of the Bible.
» You have to explain dispensational eschatology. (How do you even *pronounce* that?)

Peter is basically saying, "Share your story with people who ask." Someone may ask you questions. Someone may be curious as to why you believe what you believe. Someone may ask you what it means to be a Christian. Don't freak out. **You don't have to know everything. Just talk about what you do know.** And talk about it with "gentleness and respect."

Those last three words are huge. Sometimes it's easy to answer questions about your beliefs with judgment or anger. Peter is saying, instead, to prepare a response that comes across as gentle and respectful to whomever is asking.

Here are some steps to get prepared:

1. **Think about it.** Don't say, "I don't know." First of all, you are way too smart for that. You have so many resources right in front of you. Use that incredible brain of yours! And take some time to think through why you believe what you believe. Do some reading and research. Be informed.
2. **Talk about it.** You knew that was coming, didn't you? After all, TALK is the title of this week. But when you practice talking about what you believe and why you believe it, it helps you form your—as Peter called it—*reason.*

And you know what happens in the process? You **Know God** better. Because you are focusing on the very core of why you entered into a relationship with Him in the first place.

SO, PRACTICE TELLING YOUR STORY.

DAY 20

○ WRITE IT, EMAIL IT, SAY IT OUT LOUD—WHATEVER WORKS BEST. TALK ABOUT WHY YOU BELIEVE WHAT YOU BELIEVE. THEN, TAKE A FEW MINUTES AND COME UP WITH SOME ANSWERS TO THESE COMMON QUESTIONS. HOW WILL YOU RESPOND WITH GENTLENESS AND RESPECT?

"Why do you go to church?"

....

....

....

"Why do you pray before you eat?"

....

....

....

"Why do you read your Bible?"

....

....

....

"Why do you believe in God?"

....

....

....

"Why are you so nice to people?"

....

....

....

◔ USE THIS SPACE TO WRITE THE ANSWER(S) TO ANY QUESTION(S) YOU HAVE ALREADY BEEN ASKED OR THINK YOU COULD BE ASKED:

QUESTION(S):

....

....

....

ANSWER(S):

....

....

....

DAY 21

Tom Brady is currently the quarterback of the New England Patriots. Since he became the starting QB, the Patriots have won three Super Bowls—Brady was the MVP in two of them. He's been selected to play in eight Pro Bowls and holds the NFL record for most touchdown passes in a single regular season. His playoff win total is the highest in NFL history.

If you hate football, maybe you'll find these facts interesting: Brady is married to a Brazilian supermodel. He has hosted Saturday Night Live. He has appeared on *The Simpsons* and *Family Guy*. And he's a sponsor for Stetson Cologne. So, he smells good, too.

Oh yeah, and he makes a lot of money.

But do you know that the only reason Brady got to play in the first place is because the Pro Bowl quarterback in front of him suffered a hit that caused *internal bleeding?* Ouch! That's when Tom Brady quit *talking* and started *doing.*

A big step toward knowing God is *getting in the game.* You get off the bench, and you go where the action is. (Forgive the cheesy sports analogy.) You *use your influence.* And yes, you have influence. Whether your influence reaches the far corners of the high school stadium or seems to stop at your front door, when you **Know God,** people start to notice. And when people notice you really **Know God,** it's up to you to accurately *represent* God.

Here's how Matthew puts it:

> *"You are the light of the world. A city on a hill cannot be hidden,"* (Matthew 5:14).

Matthew references a city on a hill. Have you ever flown at night and approached a city off at a distance? That's what people do when light bursts out of darkness—they look.

Do you know someone whose world seems a little dark right now? Maybe you know someone who's making terrible decisions. Or maybe you know someone who's intelligent or eloquent, but when it comes to things of God, they just don't know. They're just . . . well, in the dark. That's what Jesus was referring to—a world full of darkness.

Into that world, Jesus sends you. In a world where the power's out, you have a flashlight. Not because you're perfect, you have it all together, or you're better than anyone. But because you've met Jesus, which means you've encountered the inventor of light. You may not be the *most* influential, but you *do* have influence—everyone does.

And sometimes that means *talking*. And sometimes that means *doing*. But the key is this: God wants to use you. **You were created to be a light in the dark.**

❯ START WITH ONE PERSON WHO NEEDS "LIGHT" IN THEIR LIFE RIGHT NOW. WRITE DOWN THEIR NAME. PRAY FOR THEM. PRAY THEY SEE THE LIGHT OF JESUS IN YOU. ASK GOD FOR OPPORTUNITIES TO TALK TO THEM, OR TO SIMPLY BE A LIGHT FOR THEM.

....

....

....

....

....

....

IF YOU WANT TO **KNOW GOD** . . .
TALK ABOUT HIM WITH YOUR FRIENDS.

|||||||||||||||||||||||||||||||||||||||||||||||||||||||||||||||||||||||||||||||||||||||||||||||||||

Before you talk to other people about God, it might help for you to take some time to think about what God has done in your life. What is your story? How has God shown up in your life to reveal who He is and how much He loves you?

◗ WRITE YOUR STORY—THE STORY OF THE WAYS GOD HAS SHOWN UP IN YOUR LIFE—HERE:

When and how did you first believe God's story?

How has God changed your life?

How has God answered prayers for you?

What has God taught you?

And you know what? These questions could be great to *talk* about with some other people who **Know God.** Ask them about their stories. Because you never know what you might learn about God when you **talk about Him with your friends.**

LIVE

Do you have people in your life who have done a lot for you? Maybe they've sacrificed for you. Provided for you. Loved you. And you know that you can't pay them back in a way that matches their kindness. But don't you wish you could do *something*?

One more question. When it comes to God:
Has God done more for you, or have you done more for God?
(We both know that answer, so you don't have to write it down.)

Paul, who wrote the book of Romans, talks a little bit about this. He basically says:

> *"Here's the thing, did you do something so incredible for God that He's up in heaven trying to express His gratitude to you? No! It's the other way around. God has actually done everything for you. He made you. He sent His Son so you could be forgiven. He made you a brand new person. So pretty much everything about you has been made for Him and Him alone." (Romans 11:35-36 Paraphrased by Kristen Ivy.)*

Get it? You were made for God.

That's a big thought. It means that everything about you is designed to *respond* to Him. You were created so that you could reflect the glory of God to the world around you. You were made to make Him more fully known.

Still not sure?

Think about this. There's something inside all of us that *wants* to worship. We have a desire to celebrate *something*. Most of us are good at getting so wrapped up in something that everyone around us sees our enthusiasm. In fact, our excitement gets some of them excited, too.

Maybe you have felt this way about:
A movie. A football team. A new band. A crush. A more-than-crush. A school dance. An item on the 99-cent menu at Wendy's.

But here's what Paul was pointing out: If you already have the urge to worship—get over-the-top excited about something, wrapped up in it, and fired up to celebrate it—**why not worship the most important thing?** The thing you were actually created to worship? Why not worship Jesus?

Paul reminds us how amazing God is. He says, really, when you think about what Jesus has done for you, you realize your whole life should be spent worshiping Him.

The book of Revelation says that in heaven, around the throne of God the Father and Jesus the Son, there are beings that literally spend all night and all day saying:

> *"Holy, holy, holy is the Lord God Almighty, who was, and is, and is to come," (Revelation 4:8).*

They get it. They're so aware of how amazing God is that they just can't stop worshiping.

So, should you start repeating that line under your breath all day and all night? No. Sure, it's not a bad idea to think it once in a while. But at some point, you're probably going to want to stop to eat a couple of Taco Bell chalupas. Or take a nap. Or play some video games. Or work on your 40-yard dash time. And God's okay with that.

What we are saying is that as you get to **Know God**, you will find that you may want to do something just to thank Him for being awesome. You might get excited about Him and want to celebrate Him with other people. You might get fired up and want to discover ways to honor Him with your life.

That's what worship is—you developing habits of praising, serving and giving. Why? Because you understand that you were—
made by God.
remade through Jesus.
created for the purpose of worshiping Him.

There's one more thing you may want to know about worship. It's contagious. The more you do it, the more you'll want to do it. And the people around you . . . yeah, they're going to catch on.

If you still aren't sure what it means to worship, that's okay. That's what the rest of this week is about. But for now, remember this: **If you want to know more about God, make Him more important than anything.**

DAY 22

In 2010, a 62-year-old University of Alabama football fan was arrested for allegedly poisoning trees on the rival campus of Auburn University. Now, these weren't just any trees; they were the university's iconic live oaks that had marked the entrance to the campus since 1930. The man responsible was charged with a class C felony and sentenced to *three* years in prison.

So, why did he do it? What would possess a person to destroy two ancient and beloved relics? *Football.* No, you read that correctly. He loved Alabama football *that* much. Guess we know why "fan" is short for "fanatic," huh?

You probably know of someone who is *really* passionate about sports. But would that person go to prison on behalf of their favorite team? Doubtful. That isn't enthusiasm or support. That's **worship**.

You worship anything that is the object of your attention and emotion. Whether you realize it or not, you *already worship something or someone*. It's true. Because *that's what you were created to do.* That's how God made you. Worshiping comes as naturally to us as eating and breathing.

> **◯ LIST THE THINGS THAT ARE CURRENTLY THE OBJECTS OF YOUR ATTENTION AND EMOTION:**

....

....

....

Here's the kicker: the God who created your attention and emotion wants your attention and emotion. He wants you to look His direction. And He wants you to give Him your passion, heart, and infatuation. And **God is worth our worship.** He deserves our attention and emotion.

The author of Psalm 95 encouraged the Israelites to worship God:

"Come, let us sing for joy to the LORD; let us shout aloud to the Rock of our salvation. Let us come before him with thanksgiving, and extol him with music and song," (Psalm 95:1-2).

Maybe if you took "LORD" and "Rock of our salvation" out of this verse and replaced them with your favorite band, celebrity, sports team, video game, or the person you're dating, you would start to understand. We worship. It's part of our DNA. And in the midst of everything competing for your worship stands the One who made you to worship in the first place.

So, why don't you take some of your attention and emotion, and place God on the receiving end of it?

❷ *FOCUS.* WRITE DOWN THREE WAYS GOD CAPTURES YOUR ATTENTION. (HERE ARE SOME EXAMPLES: A BEAUTIFUL DAY, AN UNEXPECTED BLESSING, ETC.):

1.
....

2.
....

3.
....

❷ *FEEL.* NOW, TAKE A MINUTE OR TWO AND THANK GOD. APPRECIATE HIM. DIRECT THE PASSION YOU WERE BORN WITH TOWARD THE GOD WHO MADE YOU.

(L) DAY 23

Do you love hugs or hate them? Ladies, are you the type who hugs anyone within arm's reach when you get excited? Guys, do you think you're too cool to hug it out? Or are you like those big jocks on ESPN? (All those guys ever do is hug each other!)

Whether you like hugs or not, you should probably indulge in a couple every now and then. Here's why: several years ago a team of researchers from the University of North Carolina did a study on hugging. The study concluded that hugs had several medical benefits, including reduced blood pressure. Who knew?!

A lot of Christians have this idea that they get *hug*-like approval from God when they are obedient. Like God reaches down from heaven and gives them a little squeeze. Maybe tousles their hair, even. But maybe for you, no matter how hard you try to be good enough to deserve one of those celestial embraces, 99 percent of the time you end up feeling like you fall short.

Here's where the problem lies: Sometimes we think we can *earn* God's love. We think if we obey enough, He'll approve of us. If we get rid of all our struggles, then we'll be okay with God. The truth is, **God's love is free.** Period. End of story.

Following Jesus isn't about **what I do for God**; it's about **what God has already done for me**. When Jesus died on the cross, He carried your sin. *His* death—not *your* obedience—paid for your sin.

You can't earn something that has already been given to you for free.

When we understand that, we respond with a life of obedience. Our obedience is an act of worship, not work. We don't obey to earn acceptance, we obey because we have already been accepted.

John confirms:

> *"We know that we have come to know him if we obey his commands," (1 John 2:3).*

Obedience is a response to a loving relationship, not a set of rules that earns acceptance.

✪ WRITE DOWN THIS PHRASE: *GOD LOVES ME FOR FREE.*

....

Throughout the rest of your day, thank God for that fact. Claim it as truth.

DAY 24

An online article titled "75 Day-Brightening Stories of Generosity" posted this entry by a restaurant server: "Today, I saved a woman's life using the Heimlich maneuver. And after she calmed down, finished eating, and had dessert, she left me a 600 percent tip."

Most of us can't even spell *Heimlich maneuver,* much less perform it. But for this server, their quick thinking sure brought home some cash.

Generous, right? Maybe.

Think about it. We'd probably all react the same way as the lady who choked. In light of what was done for her, leaving a 600 percent tip kind of makes sense, right? In fact, a 600 percent tip might even seem stingy in exchange for a life. (Or maybe that's all she thought her life was worth!)

What's difficult, however, is generosity without cause. It's hard to give when there's no payoff. As human beings, we aren't prone to share. Have you ever watched toddlers playing together? Their instinctive response is to cling to their own toys while simultaneously stealing the toys of kids around them. Sneaky creatures, aren't they? And be warned—if you ever steal a toy from a toddler, it can get ugly fast!

Bottom line—sharing doesn't come naturally to us. This isn't new information. Over 2,000 years ago, shortly after Jesus ascended into heaven, Paul wrote a letter to the new church in Corinth encouraging his readers to go against their natures and live a life of generosity.

"Each man should give what he has decided in his heart to give, not reluctantly or under compulsion, for God loves a cheerful giver,"
(2 Corinthians 9:7).

REWRITE THIS VERSE IN YOUR OWN WORDS:

....

....

....

Don't just give—give *cheerfully*. Give as if it's an act of worship and God will notice. According to this verse, **God loves it when we give generously.**

Instead of rejoicing in the fact that you have a whole piece of gum to yourself, rejoice in the fact that you have more than enough to share. Find *joy* and *cheer* in the simple act of finding what you have to spare and giving it away generously and without reservations.

Give.
Give cheerfully.
Give generously.

LIST THREE WAYS YOU ARE ABLE TO GIVE GENEROUSLY:

1.
....
2.
....
3.
....

DAY 25

A team of scientists determined that Tau Ceti, the star that is most similar to our sun and closest to the Earth, may have a planet in its orbit where human life could exist. They believe that the planet is in Tau Ceti's "habitable zone," meaning, "the distance of the planet from the star allows for temperatures to be at a level which would allow for life like we see on Earth." (Beichman, Charles. "Life on another planet not far, far away...maybe." www.scpr.org.)

Tau Ceti is only 12 light years away. So, you could basically jump on a spaceship (that went as fast as the speed of light) and 12 short years later you could literally be walking around in a different world.

No one knows if this planet *really* has life, but it's fun to think about—to wonder what life would be like if we could forget all we know and start over. Maybe their cars move sideways. Maybe they don't have cars at all. Maybe their cavemen invented something much cooler than the wheel and that's what all modes of transportation run on. Maybe they have figured out how to teleport and don't need transportation at all! Maybe . . . maybe this is getting a little off track.

The point is that Jesus actually talks about this idea with His friends, the 12 disciples. He talks about discovering a new way to live, and we don't even have to go to another planet to find it. It's called serving. He says:

> *"Whoever finds his life will lose it, and whoever loses his life for my sake will find it," (Matthew 10:39).*

In other words, **the way to find your life is to give it away.** *How?* You give your life away by giving away your time and talents to help someone else. You give your life away by serving.

And when you give your life away by serving, you will gain:

1. **Joy.** In 2011 there was a scientific study that focused on two groups of people who were exactly the same except for one factor—one group served regularly in their church or community. That group registered significantly higher levels of satisfaction and happiness. In fact, brain scans showed higher activity on a weekly basis in the pleasure center of their brains.

2. **Community.** Few things bring people together more effectively than serving. It has a way of deepening relationships around a common passion.

3. **Significance.** God has a way, through serving, of making our insignificant contributions significant. Serving is one way God answers the question, *"Why do I matter?"* Serving gives people purpose.

The invitation to serve is an invitation to find life like never before. It's an invitation into joy, community, significance, and intimacy with your heavenly Father. It's an invitation to a greater existence.

● NAME THREE WAYS YOU CAN SERVE. REMEMBER, SERVING CAN BE ANYTHING FROM HELPING YOUR MOM WITH THE DISHES TO VOLUNTEERING IN A WEEKLY CAPACITY IN YOUR CHURCH OR COMMUNITY.

1.
....

2.
....

3.
....

DAY 26

Do you have a job? Do you hate it? Look on the bright side! Chances are, it's not as bad as these jobs:

» **Brazilian Mosquito Researcher.** Scientists fighting malaria have to study the biting habits of the mosquitoes that spread it. The only way they can properly test the biting habits of the bugs? Let the mosquitoes bite them over and over.

» **Cat Food Quality Controller.** This job involves burying your face in a tub of cat food to test freshness, and digging through it to check for bony bits and gristle.

Now, some of you may not have a *job*, but you do have *work*. You have schoolwork. You have homework. Sports. Band. Theater. Chores. Babysitting. A volunteer position at your church. On and on we could go.

◎ WHAT "WORK" DO YOU HAVE RIGHT NOW?

....

....

....

Did you know the Bible has something to say about how we work? Listen to what Paul wrote:

"Whatever you do, work at it with all your heart, as if working for the Lord, not for men," (Colossians 3:23).

All your heart. Don't work halfheartedly. Work as if you're working for God. There's another passage in Colossians that says, "D,o it all in the name of the Lord Jesus" (Colossians 3:17). In other words, **consider your work an act of worship.** Don't see it as pointless and insignificant. See it as an opportunity.

» **Work hard.** Show up on time, prepared to give your best effort. If you're in the marching band, play the tuba like God Himself is sitting in the bleachers at half-time. If you run cross-country, run like you're running toward God's big pearly gates. (For some of us, we don't have to run very far to feel like we might meet God at any moment.) If you work at Moe's, wrap that burrito like Jesus is staring at you through the glass.

» **Have a good attitude.** When bosses, teachers, parents, coaches, directors, etc., can say about Christian students, "They have a great attitude," that's an awesome representation of God.

» **Be smart.** You don't have to be the best at everything you do, but you can always be the most competent. Be informed. Learn everything you can.

» **Pay attention.** Care about other people on your team, in your band, at your job, etc. Ask them questions. Listen to their answers. It's a huge opportunity for influence.

When you work in such a way that makes other people notice—and you do it because you represent Jesus—it points people toward the awesome God whom you follow.

❂ WRITE DOWN A COUPLE AREAS WHERE YOU COULD WORK HARDER.

....

....

....

Take some time to work at these things with more passion. Consider them an act of worship. Ask God to help you represent Him well in everything you do.

DAY 27

The world's most expensive bed is called the *Baldacchino Supreme,* created by Stuart Hughes. According to worldrecordacademy.com, one of the bed's distinct features is 236 pounds of 24-carat gold. The cost? Well over $6 million dollars.

You would think if you slept on a bed that costs $6 million, you would wake up with no acne and better muscle definition!

People are willing to put a high price tag on rest—probably because it's hard to come by these days. People are busy. And not just adults. Students have *a lot* going on, too. In a KidsHealth.com survey of 882 tweens, 90 percent said they felt stressed because they were too busy.

Now, some of you may be thinking, *"I wish I had too much going on . . . I wish I had anything going on. I'm just so bored!"* If you're in the 10 percent that doesn't feel too busy, today will still apply to you.

The writer of Psalm 46 talks about worshiping God because He protects us and takes care of us. Within that, he addresses the idea of rest:

> *"Be still, and know that I am God; I will be exalted among the nations, I will be exalted in the earth," (Psalm 46:10).*

Here are three reasons you should rest:

1. **God can handle your worries.** God is a big, strong, secure God who can handle *all* your stuff. He cares deeply and genuinely about your life. And His ability to handle your worry is different than your ability to handle it. When you invite Him to get involved in all the things that stress you out, He brings His power, plans, purpose, and ability into your world.

2. **Rest makes space for God.** Rest is not about laziness or doing nothing. It's about allowing room in your heart, mind, life, and schedule for your **relationship** with God. You can worship God and enjoy Him more when you slow down and appreciate Him.

3. **You'll work better.** You see this in other areas of your life. For all of you fitness freaks who work out constantly, you probably know that your muscles grow when you rest. It's the same in your life—you will be *more effective* in school, work, relationships (the list goes on and on), when you rest.

Bottom line, **when you trust God, you will rest**. It's not about being lazy or not working hard—we've already addressed the importance of work. It's about accepting the fact that God is in control, and intentionally creating space to worship Him as we let our minds and bodies recover.

⊘ WRITE DOWN SOME OF THE BIG PIECES OF YOUR SCHEDULE TODAY (OR TOMORROW IF IT'S LATE). CIRCLE THE PART OF THE DAY WHERE YOU'RE GOING TO WORSHIP THROUGH REST:

....

....

....

....

....

....

....

....

....

....

....

DAY 28

Asa Candler, an early president of Coca-Cola, was concerned that other companies would steal Coke's recipe. He insisted that no one ever write it down again, and shredded all documents that could possibly reveal its ingredients. (www.dailymail.co.uk)

Today, only two people alive know the formula, and the list of ingredients is locked in a bank vault. (www.dailymail.co.uk)

Coca-Cola realized something significant:
- » We have a recipe.
- » It's awesome.
- » We must hide it.

Jesus also realized something significant:
- » We have a recipe.
- » It's awesome.
- » We must NOT hide it.

When asked what was the greatest commandment in the Law, Jesus replied:

"'Love the Lord your God with all your heart and with all your soul and with all your mind.' This is the first and greatest commandment. And the second is like it: 'Love your neighbor as yourself,'" (Matthew 22:37-39).

There's the secret recipe: *love God and love others.* It's the way to **Know God,** and it's the way to make God known. In the same way that Coca-Cola's secret recipe makes them stand out, *love is what makes Jesus-followers different from the rest of the world.*

God is big and vast. He's infinite. There is so much you can learn about Him. But as you approach Him, **start with love.**

The Bible is a rich book full of incredible insights, narratives, and challenges. It is so relevant, but at times complex. You could spend your whole life studying it and never have it "figured out." So, on your journey to **Know God** better, **start with love.**

We've talked about a lot of things you can do in this journal—read and memorize Scripture, pray, live in community, talk with unbelievers, worship, work hard, rest, etc. But always **start with love.**

And not just in what you *think* or in what you *feel*—in what you *do*. **Everything we *do* should be done through the filter of love**—it is our secret formula.

As we bring this four-week journey to a close, this is our prayer for you:

God, thank You for each student who has gone through this journal. Continue to show them Your love each moment. Remind them that You are love, and that Your love never fails. Show them how to love You, Father, and teach them how to love others. In Jesus' name, amen.

AND AS YOU CONTINUE YOUR QUEST TO **KNOW GOD,**

START WITH LOVE

When you **HEAR**	When you **PRAY**	When you **TALK**	When you **LIVE**
Read the Bible through the filter of love.	Pray that God will show you how to love Him and others.	Let your conversations with believers and unbelievers be founded in love.	Let your worship be a response to God's love.

||||||||||||||||||||||||||||||||||||||||||||||||||||||||||||||||||||||||||||||||||||||

WORSHIP CAN BE PRETTY PERSONAL.

»   Some people like to worship God by singing loudly to God with their arms up in the air. Other people prefer to worship God by being very quiet.

»   Some people like to worship God with lots of other people. Others prefer to worship God by walking alone outside.

»   Some people like to dance, play an instrument or use a talent to worship God. Others like to worship God by giving money or stuff to people who can benefit from it, or by using their time and energy to serve others.

There are a lot of ways to honor God with your worship.

WHAT ARE SOME WAYS THAT YOU WORSHIP GOD BEST?